Rookie
Read-About® Math

Pen Pals Compare

By Brian Sargent

Consultant
Ari Ginsburg
Math Curriculum Specialist

Children's Press®
A Division of Scholastic Inc.
New York   Toronto   London   Auckland   Sydney
Mexico City   New Delhi   Hong Kong
Danbury, Connecticut

Designer: Herman Adler Design
Photo Researcher: Caroline Anderson
The photo on the cover shows a girl comparing the sizes of her dog and her pen pal's dog.

Library of Congress Cataloging-in-Publication Data

Sargent, Brian, 1969–
   Pen pals compare / by Brian Sargent ; consultant, Ari Ginsburg.
      p. cm. — (Rookie read-about math)
   Includes index.
   ISBN 0-516-25262-3 (lib. bdg.)   0-516-25363-8 (pbk.)
   1. Arithmetic—Juvenile literature. 2. Counting—Juvenile literature. I. Ginsburg, Ari. II. Title. III. Series.
   QA115.S27 2005
   513—dc22   2005004627

CHILDREN'S PRESS, and ROOKIE READ-ABOUT®, and associated logos are trademarks and/or registered trademarks of Scholastic Library Publishing. SCHOLASTIC and associated logos are trademarks and/or registered trademarks of Scholastic Inc.

1 2 3 4 5 6 7 8 9 10 R 14 13 12 11 10 09 08 07 06 05

Rosa and Eric are pen pals.
They write each other letters.

Rosa lives in California.
Eric lives in Texas.

They have never met.

CANADA

WASHINGTON
OREGON
MONTANA
NORTH DAKOTA
MINNESOTA
NEW HAMPSHIRE
VERMONT
MAINE
IDAHO
SOUTH DAKOTA
WISCONSIN
MICHIGAN
NEW YORK
MASSACHUSETTS
WYOMING
IOWA
PENNSYLVANIA
RHODE ISLAND
CONNECTICUT
NEW JERSEY
NEBRASKA
OHIO
DELAWARE
NEVADA
UTAH
ILLINOIS
INDIANA
WEST VIRGINIA
MARYLAND
CALIFORNIA
COLORADO
KANSAS
MISSOURI
KENTUCKY
VIRGINIA
Washington, D.C.
ARIZONA
NEW MEXICO
OKLAHOMA
ARKANSAS
TENNESSEE
NORTH CAROLINA
ALABAMA
GEORGIA
SOUTH CAROLINA
TEXAS
MISSISSIPPI
LOUISIANA
FLORIDA

North
West   East
South

ALASKA   CANADA
MEXICO
HAWAII

5

Rosa writes a question
to Eric.

"My house has one level.
How many levels does your
house have?"

Eric writes back to Rosa.

"My house has two levels. The number of levels in my house is greater than the number of levels in yours."

2 levels > 1 level

Rosa writes, "My dog weighs 150 pounds. How much does yours weigh?"

Eric writes, "My dog weighs only 6 pounds. My dog weighs less than your dog."

6 pounds < 150 pounds

14

Rosa writes, "I'm 49 inches tall. How tall are you?"

Eric writes, "I'm 50 inches tall. My height is greater than your height."

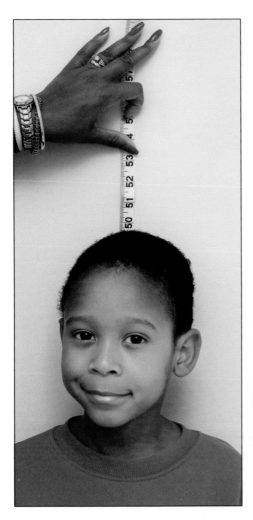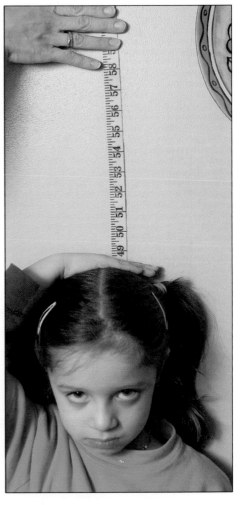

50 inches > 49 inches

18

Eric writes, "My backpack can hold three books. What about yours?"

Rosa writes, "My backpack can hold five books. It can hold more books than your backpack can."

5 books > 3 books

22

Eric writes, "I like to eat pancakes for breakfast. I always eat two pancakes.

What do you eat for breakfast?"

Rosa writes, "I like pancakes, too! I always eat one pancake.

The number of pancakes I eat is less than the number of pancakes you eat."

1 pancake < 2 pancakes

Eric writes, "I have two sisters. Do you have any brothers or sisters?"

Rosa writes, "I have two sisters, too!

The number of sisters you have is equal to the number of sisters I have!"

2 sisters = 2 sisters

Words You Know

backpack

dog

height

house

pancake

pen pal

sisters

Index

About the Author

Brian Sargent is a middle-school math teacher. He lives in Glen Ridge, New Jersey, with his wife Sharon and daughter Kathryn. He is more than thirty years old.

Photo Credits

Photographs © 2005: Bob Italiano: 5; Corbis Images/Royalty-Free: 9 bottom left, 13 top, 30 top right, 31 top left; Jay Mallin Photos: cover, 3, 6, 8, 14, 17, 18, 21, 26, 29, 30 top left, 30 bottom, 31 top right, 31 bottom right; Peter Arnold Inc./Gerard Lacz: 11, 13 bottom; PhotoEdit/Mark Richards: 7; PictureQuest: 22, 25 bottom (Benjamin F. Fink Jr.), 25 top, 31 bottom left (Spike Mafford).